Blackman

A PROFILE

Verna Wilkins
Illustrated by Virginia Gray

Tamarind

Malorie Blackman – Black Stars
TAMARIND BOOKS 978 1 848 53001 0

Published in Great Britain by Tamarind Books,
a division of Random House Children's Books
A Random House Group Company

This edition published 2008

1 3 5 7 9 10 8 6 4 2

Text copyright © Verna Wilkins 2008
Illustrations copyright © Virginia Gray

Set in Sabon

TAMARIND BOOKS
61–63 Uxbridge Road, London, W5 5SA

www.tamarindbooks.co.uk
www.kidsatrandomhouse.co.uk
www.rbooks.co.uk
Addresses for companies within The Random House Group Limited can be found at:
www.randomhouse.co.uk/offices.htm
THE RANDOM HOUSE GROUP Limited Reg. No. 954009
A CIP catalogue record for this book is available from the British Library.
Printed and bound in China

Contents

CHAPTER ONE

Family Life

BEHIND MALORIE BLACKMAN'S sparkling smile and engaging laugh lies a hardworking and successful person. Fifty of her books are in print and she is adding to that formidable list. Her books sell all over the world, and she has won many top awards.

Malorie was born at Nelson's Hospital, Merton, Surrey, England, in February, 1962. Two years previously, her parents had arrived in England from

Barbados in the Caribbean, in order to make a better life for themselves. They had left their two elder children with relatives in Barbados so that they could find jobs and set up a good home for the family in England. Just as soon as they settled down, Malorie was born.

When Malorie was three years old, her mother gave birth to twin boys. Malorie loved being a big sister and helped her mother with the new babies. The family grew to its full size when the two eldest

children, left behind in Barbados, arrived in England.

Very soon, her elder brother and sister were teaching Malorie the games they played in Barbados and Malorie taught them the ones she knew. The children were delighted when they found out that many of the games, like hide and seek, rounders and hopscotch, had exactly the same names and the same rules in both countries. Before very long, the children got used to each other and the full, happy household carried on.

CHAPTER TWO

School Days

MALORIE'S FIRST SCHOOL was Churchfields Primary School in Beckenham, Kent. Ever since her older sister and brother started going to school, she had wanted to do the same. She couldn't wait. On her very first day, she ran off into the playground without even saying goodbye to her mum.

"Can I have a look at some of those books please?" was the first question Malorie asked her teacher.

Dozens of colourful, shiny picture books were piled on two low tables. Others were stacked on shelves that covered the bottom half of one entire wall of her new classroom. Malorie was fascinated. She cried when she had to go home that afternoon.

"How was school?" her mum would ask most days as soon as Malorie got in.

"Great!" Malorie always replied. "The books are brilliant!"

Malorie was one of the first children in her class to learn to read. She wanted to spend all day, every day, in the quiet corner with her nose in a book. Her teacher, Miss Jones, had to coax her back to her desk to do her writing and other lessons.

"Come on, Malorie!" said Miss Jones. "You've read quite a lot today. Now I'd like you to write a story!"

"But I only want to read," said Malorie. "I can't think what to write!"

"Use your imagination!" said Miss Jones. "Imagine where the Moon goes during the day. Imagine where the Sun goes at night. Imagine that the stars are holes in the floor of heaven."

Even after more than thirty years, Malorie still has a vivid picture of Miss Jones encouraging her to write one, simple story in a small, chilly classroom in Kent.

CHAPTER THREE

Always Reading

BY THE TIME SHE WAS EIGHT, Malorie had read nearly all the fiction books in the school library. She could recite the first two pages of *The Silver Chair* by C.S. Lewis nearly off by heart. The Narnia Books, the Chalet stories, *Jane Eyre*, *Rebecca* and dozens of other books, sat on her bookshelf at home. They were dog-eared from Malorie's fingers turning the pages as she read them over and over again. On Saturdays, she spent hours at the local library. She must have read thousands of stories.

"That girl always has her nose in a book and her head in the clouds," her father said to her mother. "Why doesn't she read some books with facts? What's the point of fiction? It's only made-up stuff!"

"Let her be," said her mother. "She's no trouble. Maybe you could teach her to ride her new bike. That will get her out in the fresh air. The older kids have been out playing for hours!"

Her father was a good teacher and Malorie quickly learned to ride. Soon, she was tearing around the neighbourhood at great speed shouting, "I can fly! I can fly!"

Sometimes she hid her bike and climbed up into an enormous tree. In the branches, high above the

ground, she pretended she was in a world full of magical monsters and ferocious hobgoblins. She imagined some amazing adventures.

Between the ages of eight and ten Malorie was happy at home and at school. She had many friends and often made up stories and jokes that kept them all laughing. She was popular on the rounders team and played a great game of tennis. But sometimes, she would wander off, get lost in a book and completely forget about an important match.

She managed most subjects at school very well, but loved English. It was by far her best. Both parents were very proud when she passed her eleven plus exam.

"Well done, girl," said her father. "A new bike could be on the way. Congratulations!"

"Good girl," said her mother with a huge smile. "We're very proud of you."

The next term, Malorie went to Honor Oak Grammar school and settled well.

CHAPTER FOUR

Loss

IN 1975, WHEN MALORIE WAS THIRTEEN years old, her world changed dramatically. She came home from school one day to find her mother in tears.

"What's the matter, Mum?" asked Malorie.

Her mother explained that a few hours earlier, their father had left her and the children to go and live somewhere else. It was a terrible shock. Malorie's older sister and brother were grown up and had just left home, but that still left her mother to bring up Malorie and the twins. It was a difficult time for all of them. Malorie felt upset and scared and sometimes very sad.

She spent a lot of time in her bedroom listening to music. She bought a diary and wrote in it every night. The diary was very small so when she decided to write some poems, Malorie used exercise books. She wrote about all her feelings of sadness and fear.

Writing helped her to cope with missing her father. It also helped her to deal with the fact that her mother was sad and often very tired. She hid all this writing from the rest of the family.

After three difficult years, the family settled down. Then one day, just after her sixteenth birthday, her father reappeared. At first, it was difficult to get used to having him back in the home. He stayed a while and talked about coming back to the family, but it never happened. He left again and that was the last time Malorie ever saw him.

CHAPTER FIVE

Bad Advice

HOME LIFE SETTLED DOWN AGAIN. Malorie and her friends sometimes went to the pictures at weekends. Sometimes they went window shopping in Oxford Street. At other times they sat in each other's houses and listened to music. School life continued fairly smoothly.

Eventually it was time to think of the future.

"What have you got in mind to do as a job?" asked her Careers teacher.

It was 1979 and Malorie was seventeen years old.

"I'd really like to be an English teacher," replied Malorie with enthusiasm.

Miss Prendergast looked over her half glasses and gave a weak, discouraging smile. "I don't think that's a very good idea, Malorie. Why not try Business Studies or something like that."

"Because I want to do an English degree at university, Miss," argued Malorie.

"Well, I write the university references," Miss Prendergast replied, "and I'm afraid I can't give you a good reference to study English. I'm not even sure you're going to pass your English 'A' Level."

Malorie couldn't believe her ears. Her best subject was English. She enjoyed it, and she knew she was good at it. But here was Miss Prendergast, her Careers teacher, rattling on about Business Studies at a Polytechnic. A whole string of confused thoughts flashed through her head.

"Why is she saying that? Maybe I'm not as good at English as I thought... after all, she's the teacher... she should know!"

But then other thoughts came into her head. She'd never failed an English exam yet, and she wasn't about to start now. She looked at her Careers teacher and thought, "I'll show you, you old crow!"

Malorie was determined not only to pass, but to do well. But English at university was out. How could she get a place at university before her 'A' Level results were known, without a good reference?

Malorie gave up arguing, took the bad advice and applied to Huddersfield Polytechnic in Yorkshire to do a degree in Business Studies. She was accepted, and the following September she left home to start her course.

She loved living in Huddersfield and the new freedom of living away from home. But she hated every minute of her Business Studies course. It was a good course, but it wasn't the right one for her.

"How's college life, Malorie? Are you managing the work?" her mother asked anxiously when Malorie telephoned home.

Malorie didn't want to tell her mother how unhappy she was. She should never have followed the Careers teacher's advice.

Then suddenly in the middle of her first term, disaster struck.

CHAPTER SIX
Tragedy

ONE EVENING, IN HER ROOM AT COLLEGE, Malorie suddenly felt very unwell. She quickly developed terrible stomach pains. She just managed to open her door to cry for help when she doubled up in agony and crashed to the floor in the corridor.

Someone called for an ambulance and Malorie was rushed to hospital. The doctor on duty in the Accident and Emergency department sent for the surgeon and Malorie was immediately wheeled into the operating theatre where her appendix was removed. It was only then that they found out that they had made a terrible mistake. She had not needed an operation. The terrible pain was caused by sickle cell disease.

After the operation, Malorie slowly woke to the sound of voices. She managed to open one eye slightly but everything was hazy. At first, she thought she was dreaming. Then she felt the dull pain in her belly and remembered being rushed into the theatre. She could just see three people standing by the foot of her bed. Maybe two doctors and a ward sister. They were talking softly and looking at her notes. They didn't know she was awake.

"Interesting case, this one," one doctor was saying. "Came in with suspected acute appendicitis, but it's sickle cell disorder…"

"How bad?" asked the ward sister.

"Not sure yet, but she'll probably be dead before her thirtieth birthday! Terrible pity…"

His voice faded.

"They can't be talking about me!" Malorie thought

in a panic. "I can't die. I haven't done anything yet... There's too much I want to do!"

Malorie was only eighteen years old.

CHAPTER SEVEN

Sickle Cell Disorder

LATER THAT EVENING, Malorie fully awoke when her mother, her aunt and her uncle walked into the hospital ward.

"How are you feeling, my dear?" asked her mother.

"Horrid," said Malorie. "What have I got? And what is sickle cell disease? And why did I have to have this operation when I didn't need it. It hurts."

"Try not to worry, dear," said her mother. "Just concentrate on getting better and coming home. The operation was a mistake."

"I have to know Mum. What is going on?"

Malorie's mother knew her daughter well. She knew that Malorie would not have a moment's rest until she knew all she could about sickle cell disorder. And, ever since she had been a child, Malorie had always understood things best when she read about them.

"Here you are then, my child. I wrote it all down for you from the *Home Family Doctor* book."

Sickle cell disorder

Sickle cell disease is a disorder of the red blood cells.

Red blood cells carry oxygen to all parts of the body by using a protein called haemoglobin. Normal red blood cells contain only normal haemoglobin and are shaped like doughnuts. These cells are very flexible and move easily through small blood vessels.

But in sickle cell disease, the red blood cells contain sickle haemoglobin, which causes them to change to a curved (sickle) shape after oxygen is released. Sickle cells become stuck and form plugs in small blood vessels. This blockage of blood flow can damage the tissue. Because there are blood vessels in all parts of the body, damage can occur anywhere in the body...

"Mum, I don't want to read any more," said Malorie and gave her mother the notebook.

"Why don't the doctors cure me, instead of cutting me open for no reason?" Malorie asked.

"I'm sorry my dear," said her mum gently, "but there is no cure. Most of the time you will be perfectly well. Anyway, if you get a crisis, like you did yesterday, it can be managed quickly, now that they know what the problem is."

"What can I do to avoid a crisis?" asked Malorie.

"You should try not to get too hot or too cold," said her mum. "You should also try to drink lots of liquid so you don't become dehydrated. There are other things you can do as well. Get over this operation first and then we can really begin to sort you out."

CHAPTER EIGHT
World of Work

MALORIE STAYED IN HOSPITAL until she was well enough to travel. Then she went back home to London and her mother. Gradually, Malorie came to accept her condition and remembered to take daily doses of penicillin to keep her well. Eventually, she began to learn to live with sickle cell disorder and to lead a fairly normal life. She decided not to return to her Business Studies course.

She applied to Goldsmith's College in London to do a degree in English and Drama. She had passed all the three 'A' Level exams she had taken, English included – and she didn't need to rely on a reference from her Careers teacher to get into college.

Goldsmith's accepted her, but she decided to take a year off before starting her course, to work and earn some money.

Her first job was with a computer software company. She'd never seen a real computer before. Within a couple of weeks of starting the job, she was hooked.

Before the year was over, she knew that she wanted to carry on working with computers. She gave up her

place at Goldsmith's and worked hard at her job. She attended evening classes to gain qualifications in Computer Programming.

Over the following ten years, she changed companies three times, and eventually became a manager with Reuters, a large international company.

However, even though she was making a very good living, Malorie realised that computing wasn't enough. She was desperate to do something more creative. But what?

CHAPTER NINE

World of Writing

MALORIE HAD LONG SINCE abandoned her exercise books of poems and her diary, but she still loved reading. While many of her friends loved clothes shopping, Malorie could not go past a book shop without stopping, browsing and buying.

One day she wandered into the children's section of a very large book store. There were a few books of poetry on the shelves, and thousands of picture books.

Many were characters Malorie remembered from her own early reading. There was Snow White and Rapunzel, Red Riding Hood and Dick Whittington. There was Heidi and the Narnia characters, the Chalet girls and Dickens.

As she browsed, a sudden thought struck her. "Wouldn't it be wonderful to write some books of my own!"

Soon, she started to write again. This time she wrote stories and she wrote them on her computer. Often, she would come home from work, have a quick meal and sit tapping away for hours, her head beyond the clouds, gazing out at the stars and remembering them as holes in the floor of heaven. She hadn't thought of the stars in that way for a long, long time.

Sometimes, Malorie got so wrapped up in a story, she would write through the night. So many times she would jump out of her chair and dive into bed muttering, "Oh no! It's daylight already and I haven't even slept yet!"

She would get only a couple of hours of sleep, before having to get up again for work. Because her sleep patterns became so confused, she had terrible dreams. Many of the stories she wrote at that time were about nightmares... very scary!

CHAPTER TEN

Who's in the Picture

WHEN MALORIE MADE UP CHARACTERS for her stories, she imagined herself and people like herself as the heroes.

She had realised from a very early age that none of the books she had ever read – right from early picture books and school books in childhood – featured black children. It was only in her late twenties that she found books in some libraries and in a few bookshops written by black writers who wrote about

the lives of black people. None of the writers were British, but they became her role models. She discovered, with delight, Toni Morrison, Alice Walker, Maya Angelou, Buchi Emecheta, Terry MacMillan and James Baldwin.

She felt proud when she read that Alice Walker, and later Toni Morrison,

had won the Pulitzer prize, a top ranking award in America, for their writing. She was delighted when she read that James Baldwin's book, *Another Country*, had sold millions of copies and a film, based on his book, had been made.

Malorie realised that it was important for black children to see children like themselves in books, taking part in adventures, going about their everyday lives, laughing, crying, living, loving and just being.

Malorie continued to write. She was determined to put black children into books. She remembered all too vividly how it felt to read all those thousands of books when she was at school and not see herself once. She remembered only too well how lonely it felt to be ignored and invisible.

CHAPTER ELEVEN

Rejection

MALORIE MADE A PLAN. She worked very hard at sixteen short stories and decided to see whether she could get any of them published.

She went to the local library and asked the librarian at the information desk how to find out about publishers and publishing. The librarian gave her a copy of the *Writers' and Artists' Yearbook*, which includes all publishers in the United Kingdom. Malorie copied out the names and addresses of all the children's book publishers she could find and sent off copies of her stories to them, with a stamped addressed envelope.

Every morning when she heard the postman arrive, Malorie would charge down the stairs, hoping and praying that a publisher would have said yes to one of her stories. But none ever did. She received rejection letter after rejection letter.

She was dreadfully disappointed, but she never stopped writing. One day, she read in an article in the newspaper that James Herriot, the famous author of a series of books about a vet, had received over eighty rejection letters before his first book was published. His books eventually became a highly successful television series. It gave her hope to keep on going.

One day, Malorie arrived home after work to find yet another letter from a publisher.

"Another rejection," she grumbled, tearing the envelope open.

CHAPTER TWELVE
Getting Published

THE LETTER BEGAN... Dear Malorie, we would love to publish your collection of short stories.

Malorie screamed with shock, gave a great whoop of delight and danced the funky chicken in the hall! The publisher loved the stories she had sent to them three months previously. She had written the stories for young adults, based on some nightmares she'd had and had called the collection *Not So Stupid!* After eighty-two rejection letters, a publisher had finally said "YES!"

Success was not that easy. Malorie had to re-write great chunks of her stories in order to get them just right for publishing. She was more than happy to chop and change her stories as requested by the publisher, but would always insist that the main characters in her stories are black. The vast majority of stories feature white characters and Malorie's commitment is to equality.

"My stories are not just stories for black children because the main characters are black," smiles Malorie. "The vast numbers of stories with white characters are seen as stories for everyone. By the same token, my stories are for everyone." And so they are. They sell internationally.

In order to work on her writing skills Malorie joined a Writing for Children Workshop. Each member of the group took turns to have their stories read and everyone else was invited to comment on what they liked or disliked about each story. It was hard work and very nerve-wracking. But her work improved by leaps and bounds. Soon Malorie was given a contract by the publisher. Finally in November 1990, her first collection of stories, *Not So Stupid!* came out.

Malorie was a published author. She gave up her job in computing.

During the next four years, she wrote many stories including *Hacker*, *Operation Gadgetman*, *Whizziwig*, *Pig-Heart Boy* and the Betsey Biggalow series.

Hacker, an international bestseller, won the *Young Telegraph* Children's Book of the Year Award 1994 and the WH Smith Mind Boggling Award in the same year.

CHAPTER THIRTEEN
A New Way of Life

BEING AN AUTHOR meant adjusting to a new way of working. At first it was strange not having to rush out of the house every morning to go to work. But Malorie faced a new challenge. She had to get used to motivating herself to work on her own. Then she had to get used to saying "No" when she was asked to do more work than she could manage. The life of a popular writer can be very demanding.

In 1993 Malorie applied to the National Film and Television School in order to acquire new skills. During the interview for acceptance to the school, she was asked what films she liked.

"I really enjoyed *Babette's Feast*," said Malorie.

The interviewer remarked that it was a serious and complicated film. "But I also enjoyed *Terminator* and *Lethal Weapon*," Malorie added quickly, and then immediately regretted having mentioned such violent films.

She needn't have worried. She was accepted and thoroughly enjoyed the course.

At the end of the course, Malorie teamed up with a director and made a film called *Play Time*.

The film was based on a real experience she had in her third year of junior school. Malorie had to move from a small local school to a larger one, in Lewisham.

It was a real shock. A tough gang reigned at the new school. Gina, the gang leader, was mean and hard. Every newcomer was a natural victim for the gang. Gina selected one of her followers to fight each new girl who arrived.

One afternoon after school, in the local park, Malorie was surrounded by the gang.

"Hit her!" one voice chanted. Malorie was petrified. All of a sudden a blow landed on her shoulder. She was stunned for a moment, but then lashed out at her opponent. She was no great fighter and she was soundly beaten. The gang swaggered off with Gina grinning and leading them down the road. Malorie went home bruised, shaken and upset.

It took her quite a long time to settle and make friends at the school, but eventually she did.

Then the tables turned. Someone spread some horrible rumours through the school about Gina's dad. The gang deserted her and the once so fierce Gina became a sad, lonely creature.

The film was action packed and a great success.

CHAPTER FOURTEEN

An Interview with Malorie Blackman

Verna Wilkins: Malorie, do you enjoy writing?

Malorie Blackman: I love it. I can't imagine ever doing anything else now.

VW: Does your sickle cell disorder stop you from writing?

MB: Nope! Obviously when I'm ill or in pain, I tend not to work. I've got a computer program that lets me dictate stories straight into a file, just in case I have a crisis where my hands swell up and I can't use them.

Shall I tell you a funny story – well, I thought it was funny! A friend's young daughter asked why I was using the voice dictation program and not typing. (I wasn't ill. I was just trying it out for size!) I explained about my sickle cell. My friend's daughter then told her mum that I had "sick-as-hell disease". That made me laugh like a drain.

VW: How do you maintain such a wonderful sense of humour?

MB: Do I? If I do, it's because I try to see the funny side of most things. And loving what I do helps to cheer me up, even if I'm feeling low.

VW: Do you ever get lonely? Sitting alone in front of a computer must be a lonely business!

MB: Sometimes. I spend quite a lot of time in a back bedroom, but luckily I like my own company! Besides which, with all the characters I love to make up, how could I be lonely for long! It's as if all my characters become real people to me whilst I'm writing about them. Also, my publishers keep me on the run and get me out and about.

VW: Do you have any hobbies?

MB: I have a number of hobbies. Reading is the one I love best. I love books. I don't think I could write if I didn't read. And I love music. We have a saxophone, a piano, a recorder, a drum kit and two guitars in our house – and I play all of them badly! But I am taking piano lessons. I also love computer games. I play on my PC or my Playstation or my Nintendo console… Yes! I admit it – I've got all three! Isn't that sad? I also like country walks and I love the sea. One day, I'd love to be able to live by the sea.

VW: Where do you get inspiration for all those wonderful books – how many to date?

MB: Fifty and growing! The inspiration for my writing comes from anywhere and everywhere. I keep my eyes and ears open and I must admit, being nosy is a great help. I've always been nosy, but now I say – it's research! Isn't that a great excuse for peering into other people's houses? It's research!

VW: Thank you for bringing so much pleasure and inspiration to so many thousands of readers.

Books and Prizes

GIRL WONDER SERIES:
Girl Wonder and the Terrific Twins – Gollancz, 1991; Puffin (pb)
Girl Wonder's Winter Adventures – Gollancz, 1991 (out of print); Puffin (pb)
Girl Wonder to the Rescue – Gollancz, 1994; Puffin (pb)

BETSEY BIGGALOW SERIES:
Betsey Biggalow Is Here! – Piccadilly, 1992; Mammoth (pb)
Betsey Biggalow, the Detective – Piccadilly, 1992; Mammoth (pb)
Hurricane Betsey – Piccadilly, 1993; Mammoth (pb)
Magic Betsey – Piccadilly, 1994; Mammoth (pb)
Betsey's Birthday Surprise – Piccadilly, 1996; Mammoth (pb)

PICTURE BOOKS:
That New Dress – Simon & Schuster, 1991 (out of print)
Mrs Spoon's Family – Andersen, 1995
The Marty Monster – Tamarind, 1999
Dizzy's Walk – Tamarind, 1999
Where's My Cuddle? – Orchard, 2001
Jessica Strange – Hodder, 2001

BOOKS FOR YOUNGER CHILDREN:
Elaine, You're not a Brat! – Orchard, 1991
My Friend's a Gris-Quick! – Scholastic, 1994
Rachel Versus Bonecrusher the Mighty – Longman Education, 1994
Rachel and the Difference Thief – Longman Education, 1994
Jack Sweettooth the 73rd! – Viking, 1995

Grandma Gertie's Haunted Handbag – Heinemann, 1996
The Secret of the Terrible Hand – Orchard, 1996
Peril on Planet Pellia – Orchard, 1996
Mystery on the Mellian Moon – Orchard, 1996
The Quazar Quartz – Orchard, 1996
Space Race – Young Corgi, 1997
Fangs – Orchard, 1998
Aesop's Fables – Scholastic, 1998
The Snow Dog – Transworld/Corgi Pups, 2000

NOVELS:
Hacker – Doubleday, 1992; Corgi (pb)
Operation Gadgetman – Doubleday, 1993; Yearling (pb); TV
film by Hallmark Films/Scottish TV
Thief! – Doubleday, 1995, Corgi (pb)
Deadly Dare – Scholastic, 1995
Whizziwig – Viking, 1995; Puffin (pb)
The Space Stowaway – Ginn, 1995
A.N.T.I.D.O.T.E. – Doubleday, 1996; Corgi (pb)
Computer Ghost – Scholastic, 1997
Don't Be Afraid – Ginn, 1997
Pig-Heart Boy – Doubleday, 1997; Corgi (pb), shown on BBC
TV 1999
Lie Detectives – Scholastic, 1998
Words Last Forever – Reed, 1998
Whizziwig Returns – Puffin, 1999
Hostage – Barrington Stoke, 1999
Dangerous Reality – Doubleday, 1999
Tell Me No Lies – Macmillan, 1999
Forbidden Game – Puffin, 1999
Animal Avengers – Egmont, 1999
Noughts and Crosses – Transworld, 1999

BOOKS FOR 14 PLUS AGE GROUP:
Not So Stupid! – Livewire/Women's Press, 1990
Trust Me – Livewire/Women's Press, 1992

TV/FILM/THEATRE SCRIPTS:
Good Company – NFTS, TV drama
Play Time – NFTS, Graduation film
Teamwork – BBC Schools Programme, TV drama
Thief!- Channel 4 Schools
Jevan – Children's ITV, drama
Whizziwig – ITV 3 series
The Lost Puzzle of Gondwana – Libretto written for Southwark Festival
Pig-Heart Boy – BBC1, 6-part serial

PRIZES:
WH Smith Children's Book of the Year Award 1994 for *Hacker*
Young Telegraph Children's Book of the Year Award 1994 for *Hacker*
Young Telegraph Children's Book of the Year Award for *Thief!*
Stockport Children's Book of the Year Award 1997 for *A.N.T.I.D.O.T.E.*
Voice/Excelle Children's Writer of the Year Award 1997
UKRA Award 1998 for *Pig-Heart Boy*
Shortlisted for Carnegie Medal 1998 for *Pig-Heart Boy*
Play Time won a Certificate of Merit at the 31st Chicago International Film Festival

Malorie has also been shortlisted for a number of other prizes.